Saint Vincent, Friend of the Poor

KIMBERLY VARELA

Illustrations by

Meg Ross

ISBN:
ISBN-10: 1477447377
ISBN-13: 978-1477447376

DEDICATION

To my loving husband, Dennis. Thank you for your
encouragement.

CONTENTS

ACKNOWLEDGMENTS

Thank you Meg for the wonderful illustrations. I would also like to thank Belinda, Loretta and my son Cody for their help with the editing of this book.

CHAPTER 1

THE FARM BOY

A long time ago, in a small town in the land of France, there lived a farm boy named Vincent. He was a plain looking boy who wore shabby clothes with many patches. His family was poor. They lived in a small house near a big oak tree. His father was a farmer, his mother took care of the family, and he had three brothers and two sisters. Little Vincent had a talent for making everyone his friend because he had a good heart and truly cared about others. Vincent liked to help his Papa on the farm by taking care of the sheep and pigs.

Vincent lived near the village of Pouy where it rained quite often. When he would go out and take care of the sheep he would wear a large cape to keep from getting wet. One rainy evening, as Vincent put the last sheep back in the pen, his Mama called,

"Vincent, supper is ready!"

"I will see you again soon, my friends." He told the sheep.

He shut the gate and ran home along a rocky path. His stomach was empty, and it was getting dark and cold outside. Vincent was soaked to the bone from the rain. After he opened the door he pulled off his muddy boots and lined them up next to his brothers' boots. He hung his dripping cape on a hook by the door and went in to see his mama.

"It smells good, Mama." He said, as he kissed her on the cheek.

"This soup will make you warm." Mama said, ladling a spoonful into a small bowl.

Vincent sat down at the table with his family to eat. Papa blessed the food.

"How were the sheep today, Vincent?" asked Papa.

"The sheep were fine, Papa, but I am tired. I walked over many hills today," said Vincent.

"Thank you for working so hard, Vincent. By the way, I have good news for you," he said with a grin. "You are finally going to school."

"Really?" Vincent cried, jumping up from his chair.

Vincent was so happy. He had waited a long time for this day to come. After supper, the family knelt down by the warm fireplace to give thanks. As always, Papa led the rosary. Vincent tried to think about Jesus and Mary as he prayed, but he was too excited about school.

"I am going to school. Thank you, God!" he thought to himself.

The other children in the family knew Vincent was lucky too. School would cost too much for all of them to go. Vincent was to be a man of God, and Papa wanted him to learn.

CHAPTER 2

A HARD LESSON

There weren't any schools near the farm where Vincent lived, so he had to go to school in Pouy, which was miles away. During the week, he lived in a house with the other boys at the school, and went home on weekends and holidays. The school was too far from home to make the trip every day. Vincent liked school very much and studied hard. He made new friends but still missed his family and his life on the farm.

One spring day while Vincent was in class his teacher was reading a story from the Bible about Jesus. The teacher read, "Jesus told the disciples, unless you become like a little child, you will not enter the kingdom of God." "What do you think Jesus was saying? What must we do to enter heaven?" the teacher asked the class.

Vincent raised his hand. "Yes, Vincent?" asked the teacher.

"Be small, like a child," answered Vincent.

"You're right! We must not be too proud. Good answer!" his teacher praised.

Vincent had learned from his teachers that he must not think he was better than others. He had to be humble, not proud to serve God. This was not easy for Vincent even though he was a humble person; he wanted to fit in with the other boys. Many of the other boys at the school were rich, and Vincent was poor. Their parents wore rich clothes and lived in big houses, while Vincent's family lived in a little house in the country.

One day God put Vincent to the test when Papa came to visit Vincent at school. Vincent saw Papa in the distance walking toward the school. He was limping and wearing ragged looking clothes. Vincent felt ashamed of the way his father looked, so he ran and hid until he knew his father had gone.

"I don't want my friends to see Papa," thought Vincent. "They will laugh at him."

Being humble was difficult. Vincent went to bed that night feeling very sad.

"I will tell Papa that I am sorry," he thought before he fell asleep.

CHAPTER 3

VINCENT GROWS UP

A few years later, when Vincent was a teenager, he was ready to go to the seminary, which is a special school for priests. He had done well in his first school, and his papa was very proud. Papa knew that this new school would cost even more money than his first school and it was further away. Vincent's papa knew he would have to sell something special to pay for the new school.

Papa leaned on the fence looking at his two best cows, Ginger and Daisy, whom he loved very much.

"I do not want to sell them," Papa told his neighbor, "but we need the money for Vincent to keep going to school."

"Let me buy them from you. The money will help pay for your son to go to school to become a priest and God will bless us both for helping him become a man of God," said the neighbor.

Papa felt very sad that he had to sell his cows to his neighbor. He did not want to sell Ginger and Daisy because he needed them on the farm to produce milk and plow the fields. Also, it was known that this neighbor did not always treat his animals kindly. He was the only one around who had enough money to afford them. As Papa limped slowly back to the house, he heard the crack of a whip. He kept walking and refused to turn for he knew all too well that the sound meant that the man was beating the cows. A tear fell slowly down Papa's cheek.

Later that summer, while Vincent was home from his studies, Papa gave Vincent the money for his new school.

"Papa, how did you get it?" asked Vincent.

"I sold Ginger and Daisy." Papa sighed.

Vincent felt awful. He knew that Papa loved those cows, but he also knew how much Papa wanted him to become a priest, so Vincent took the money, vowing to make his papa proud.

"I will pay him back," he thought. "Thank you Papa!" was all he said.

Later that night, Papa handed the rosary to Vincent after supper.

"You lead tonight, son."

This surprised Vincent since Papa had always led the rosary. All the children looked up to Vincent with joy and awe. Vincent was not a boy anymore. He was a man. "In the name of the Father, the Son and the Holy Spirit, Amen." Vincent prayed. Mary, his smallest sister, fell asleep at Mama's knees before he had finished the last Hail Mary. Vincent did not know that this would be the last night he would ever spend at home.

CHAPTER 4

PAPA GOES TO HEAVEN

Vincent worked hard at school and learned all he could about God and the Church. He got a job teaching children after school to make money to pay Papa back for the two cows.

"I will send the money home soon. Papa will be able to buy more cows to work his farm," thought Vincent as he lay in his bed smiling and thinking about home.

The next day Vincent got a letter from home. As he scrambled to open it he found that it had some money in it. It read:

Dear Vincent   *February 15, 1597*

Papa went to heaven today. He wanted you to have this money for school. Papa asked us to keep working hard to help you pay for school. We will send as much as we can to help you each month.

Love,

Mama

Vincent put the letter down and cried. Then he knelt down and prayed to help Papa's soul to go to heaven.

Vincent kept studying and working his hardest. He missed his family, but did not have enough money to go home and visit them. During the summers, Vincent became a tutor for other boys who wanted to become priests. The gentleman who gave him the job was so happy with his work that one day he told him, "Vincent, the boys are learning so much from you. They want to return with you to your school and keep learning from you all year."

Vincent thought for a moment. The extra money would help him to pay for school. He would have to work twice as hard as usual. It wouldn't be easy taking classes, teaching the boys and studying all night. Vincent wasn't afraid of hard work.

"Sir, I'll do it!" he told the gentleman.

Back at school, Vincent helped the boys so much that soon other boys wanted to learn from him. He decided to open a small school where he could teach all the boys. During these years at school,

Vincent prayed for his family and wrote them letters every day.

After a few more years of studying and teaching, Vincent finally made Papa's dream come true. He became a priest, a real man of God. There were only two people present at Vincent's first mass, another priest and a worker from the church, but Vincent was sure that Papa was smiling down at him from Heaven that day too.

CHAPTER 5

PIRATES

Now that Vincent was a priest, he was looking forward to serving God in his first church. He liked to wear his black robe. People knew he was a priest, and they smiled and were friendly to him.

One hot summer day, Father Vincent and his schoolmate, Goddard, were traveling home together. The two friends were discussing whether they should take a ship from Marseilles, the nearest coastal city or go by land. If they went by ship, it would save them money, but it was more dangerous because there had been many pirate attacks on the coast of Marseilles.

"Father Vincent, let's sail on a ship," said Goddard.

"Yes, that will be more fun, and it will save us some money," agreed Fr. Vincent.

The two men boarded a ship named *The Louise*. The ship had not sailed far when a guard with a scope yelled, "Three pirate ships!" Before Fr. Vincent knew what was happening, pirates were jumping from their ships and swinging from ropes onto *The Louise*. The crew from *The Louise* tried to fight back, but was outnumbered by the pirates who had very dark skin and wore rings in their noses.

"Ahh!" screamed Fr. Vincent as he was shoved down to the floor.

An arrow went into his leg and he could not get up. He watched in horror as the cruel pirates sliced down Goddard with their swords. Father Vincent closed his eyes so he couldn't watch the killings, but Goddard's screams made chills go up and down his spine.

One of the pirates grabbed Father Vincent and jerked the arrow out of his leg. Pain rushed through him as the pirate roughly pushed him across the plank to the pirate ship. The pirates were very mean to him and the other prisoners, but the worst thing to Fr. Vincent was that they made him take off his black robe.

"Put on these white pants and this cap!" yelled one large pirate with a patch over his eye.

Fr. Vincent did as he was told.

"Now nobody will know I am a priest," Father Vincent thought sadly. He was afraid of what the pirates were going to do to him and the other prisoners.

The pirates sailed the ship to the far off land of Africa. When they got there the pirates sold Fr. Vincent as a slave to a fisherman. Luckily, on his first day of fishing Father Vincent got so seasick that his master sold him back to the slavers. His next master was a scientist. The scientist soon realized what a prize he had bought. He could see that Father Vincent was holy and smart. This master was a gentleman and treated Father Vincent kindly. He believed in God, but he was not a Christian. He did not believe that Jesus was the Son of God. He wanted to teach Father Vincent about his religion, and he hoped that Father Vincent would leave his Catholic faith.

As a slave, Father Vincent had to work hard and he never made any money. He could not go home either. He had no freedom. He was very sad that he was not able to serve God as a priest, but he was thankful that his master was a kind hearted man. Every day Fr. Vincent asked the Blessed Mother to help free him.

He would silently pray as he was working, "Hail Mary, full of grace, the Lord is with Thee. Blessed art thou among women, and blessed is the fruit of thy womb, Jesus." One warm day, as Fr. Vincent was working, his master said to him, "Your God has left you. You should believe in a different God."

"He has not left me. He is testing me. I have faith in Him alone." Fr. Vincent spoke with a sincere heart.

A year later his master, the scientist, died and Fr. Vincent was sold again. This time he had to do backbreaking work all day in the fields, but he never complained and always had a kind word to say. By his example, he led other slaves to Jesus. Even his new master stopped believing in his false god and began to see that the truth and the light was Jesus.

One hot day his master told him that he was going to let Fr. Vincent go free. After nine months he kept his promise, and he and Fr. Vincent sailed back to France in a small boat. It was a dangerous trip because they could have been captured by pirates again, but God protected them. When they finally reached France, his master gave him his freedom.

Father Vincent cried, "Thank you Lord, for hearing my prayers!"

CHAPTER 6

VINCENT HELPS THE POOR

When Father Vincent arrived in France, he headed for Paris, the biggest city. It was there that he learned that God wanted him to help and serve the poor. First, he worked in a hospital. Back then, some people got an awful sickness called the plague. The plague was very painful and deadly and it was also easy to catch. If a person got the plague; they were taken away from their family to a hospital. It was hard to find nurses and doctors to work in these hospitals because nobody wanted to catch the plague. Vincent wrote a letter to

24

Mama about working in the hospital. It read:

Dear Mama   *March 12, 1609*

Hello, how are you? I miss you and hope to visit you and Mary soon. I do not have my own church yet, so I am working in a hospital in Paris. Most of the sick people have the plague. There are so many sick people and not many beds for them. There is not very much food to give them, either. The sick are men, women, children and even babies. The hospital is very dirty because we cannot find many workers. The few doctors and nurses that we have cannot do all the work, so I help them the best I can. Most days I help care for the sick. I clean their sores and give them kind words. I bless them and listen to their stories. I also mop up the dirty floors. Don't worry about me, though. God is with me and I am not afraid of catching the plague. Helping others is more important than helping myself. In helping the sick ones, I am serving Jesus. Give Mary a kiss from me. I love you and God bless!

Your son,

Vincent

CHAPTER 7

FATHER VINCENT'S FIRST CHURCH

In 1612, Father Vincent was sent to his first church. It was in the country in a town called Clichy. He was very happy as he walked into the town. Then he walked into the church, and he was shocked to see what a mess it was. There was dirt and straw on the floor. Chickens and pigs were living there. Statues were broken and the altar was dirty.

He left the church sadly, and went to find someone that lived in the town. As he came to the first door, he saw that it had boards nailed across it. It could not be opened. Suddenly he was hit in the back by a rock! Then another one hit him on the shoulder. Someone was throwing rocks at him from the second floor. He ran to another door, and the same thing happened. This time he was hit in the head.

He finally yelled at them, "Stop throwing rocks, I am your priest!" He banged on another door and was let in.

"What is going on in this town?" Father Vincent asked the man inside. "Why are all the houses boarded up?"

"There is a woman here in town that has the plague, so we all locked ourselves in our houses," said the man. "We will wait for three days until she is dead. Then we will come out."

"Where is this woman with the plague?" asked Father Vincent.

"She is in the little house at the end of the block," the man told the priest. "Don't go there or you will catch it, too."

Fr. Vincent ran to the little house. It was boarded up as well, and now many rocks were being thrown at him. He quickly removed the boards and kicked in the door. The house was dark and cold inside. Two dogs started barking at him. The poor woman had been locked in and left to die with her dogs. He found her in her bed, already dead. Then he heard a soft crying sound. In the corner was a little girl huddled on the floor. She had a blanket wrapped around her.

She looked dirty and was shivering from the cold. It must have been the dead woman's daughter. When the girl saw Father Vincent, she got up, ran to him and put her arms around him. Then he carried her out of the house and ran down the street.

On Sunday, Father Vincent had a funeral for the woman who had died. All of the town's people came out to see what was going on. After he had buried the woman, he said to the people, "As you can see, I am still alive. The woman did not have the plague. You left her daughter to be eaten by the dogs. Now she has no mother. Who will take care of her?"

A mother with five children stepped up, and said she would take the girl even though they were poor. Father Vincent smiled. There was hope in this town.

It was a big job to clean the church. Father Vincent started to do it by himself. One by one the women in the town showed up to help him. Then the men came with hammers. In a few days, it was ready for mass.

God blessed Father Vincent with the gift of being able to touch people's hearts with his words. One day at mass, he told the people about a poor family outside of town that had no food. After mass when he was going to check on the family, the road was full of people bringing food to them. That night he decided to open a soup kitchen, a place where the poor could come and eat. Father Vincent fed the poor every day with the help of some rich, kind people from Clichy and from Paris. Within a year, the people of Clichy had completely changed.

Father Vincent said, "I believe that not even the Pope is as lucky a priest as I. These people have such good hearts."

After only a year and a half at Clichy, Father Vincent had to leave his beloved first church to go somewhere else he did not want to go.

CHAPTER 8

THE TUTOR

The people of Clichy were sad to see Father Vincent go, but when a new priest came to take his place, they promised to keep going to mass. Father Vincent did not want to leave Clichy, but he needed to obey the Church and God. He was sent by the Catholic Church to a rich family's house to tutor a seven year old boy named Pierre. Pierre was a hard student to teach. He just wanted to play sports and get into trouble.

One day while Father Vincent was trying to teach Pierre his lessons, Pierre whined, "This is boring. Can I go play ball?"

"You can play in a while Pierre. Let's finish reading. What did Jesus say about loving your enemies in the gospel of Luke?" asked Fr. Vincent patiently.

"I don't care about that." Pierre said, slamming his book shut. "I just want to play!"

Just then Pierre's mom came in with Pierre's little two year old brother, Henri. Pierre got out of his chair and ran over to Henri. He grabbed him, and they started wrestling on the floor. Then they ran out the door and down the hall.

Everybody called Pierre's mom "Madame" because she was very rich and noble. She wore beautiful clothes and had soft hands.

She loved God with all her heart but was used to getting her own way.

"Oh Madame," said Father Vincent, "Pierre is learning very little. Maybe I am not a good teacher. If you wish to find someone better..."

Madame's face turned white. "Please don't leave us, Father!" she cried, and fell to her knees. "You are perfect. I want my boys to become saints more than anything else."

He turned and left the room. He decided that if Pierre did not do better soon, he would ask the Church to let him leave. At the time, Father Vincent did not know that God was going to use Madame to help him to do his greatest work.

CHAPTER 9

VINCENT'S FIRST MIRACLE

A couple of months later, Father Vincent saw that Pierre was still not learning so he went to tell Madame that he should leave. When he found Madame, she was dressed in a plain, wool dress instead of her usual fancy clothes.

Madame quickly said to Fr. Vincent, "There is much work to be done."

"What is there to do? Your son is not learning." Father sighed.

"Come with me and see," she said, taking his arm.

They traveled all over the farms and towns that day. They nursed the sick and taught the poor people about God. Father Vincent had no idea that there were so many people in need. There was enough work for ten priests. Father Vincent and Madame kept up this work for a year. Every day they went to a different town or farm to help the poor.

One snowy winter day in 1617, when Father Vincent was 35 years old, a miracle happened. He was preaching at a church in a town called Folleville. The church was packed with people. He was telling the people how important it was to confess their sins.

"Brothers and Sisters, make your hearts clean. The kingdom of God is upon us. Confess your sins and be free!"

Madame had asked him to preach about this because she knew that most of the people there hardly ever went to confession. The reason that they did not go to confession was because the priests did not teach them to go. After mass was over, every person stayed for confession! The line of people waiting to confess their sins went out the church and down the street! The people did not care that it was freezing outside.

"You cannot hear all of them by yourself, Father!" exclaimed Madame. "I will send for more priests."

When the priests came, they were shocked. Nothing like this had ever happened before. All the priests heard confessions all day long. When the people were done confessing, they went and told their friends and families, and they came to confess their sins too. It was Father Vincent's first miracle.

CHAPTER 10

THE GALLEYS

One day as Father Vincent was going about his work, he thought about the words of Jesus in the Gospel of Matthew, "I was a stranger and you did not welcome me, naked and you did not clothe me, sick and in prison and you did not visit me....Truly, I say to you, as you did it not to one of the least of these, you did it not to me."

"I will go and visit the prisoners today in the galleys," he decided.

The galleys were the prisons for the men who rowed the big ships. Back then ships were not run by steam; men had to row them. They used prisoners to do this work because it was so difficult. The prisoners were chained to their seats night and day and beaten by a whip if they stopped rowing. Many men died in their seats from weakness due to the heat and backbreaking work. When the prisoners were not rowing the ships, they lived in underground galley prisons.

When Father Vincent went to visit the prison, he was let in by a guard called the keeper. The keeper led him down deep underground. It was so dark that the keeper had to light a torch to see. The deeper they went, the colder it got.

"I don't know any of their names. We are not told who they are." The keeper told him. "Are you sure you want to do this? The smell is awful down here."

"Yes, let me in with them." Father Vincent held his breath as the keeper unlocked the gate.

To Father Vincent's horror, the prisoners started yelling curses at him from the walls they were chained to. They could not sit or stand, but were forced to crouch with their necks, hands and legs chained to the wall. The ones that were asleep were hanging from their chains. On the floor, rats were crawling around on the filthy straw. Father Vincent nearly fainted from shock. He had no idea that the galley prisoners were living like this. When he caught his breath again, he took out his crucifix, showed it to the prisoners and said,

"This man knows what it means to suffer too. He died for our sins even though he was innocent."

"Let me see that!" growled one of the prisoners.

Carefully, Father Vincent put the crucifix close to the prisoner's face so he could see

Jesus on the cross. The crazy look in his eyes left him, and he started to cry. Each man wanted to see the crucifix, and all of them were moved to tears at the sight of it.

"I will come again tomorrow, my dear brothers, and bring bread for you." Father Vincent promised as he left.

The next day, Father Vincent did as he promised, and brought food for the hungry men. He spent the whole day with them, nursing their wounds and talking to them about God and his Son, Jesus. He wrote down their names and wrote letters for them, which he gave to their families. He came everyday to the prison, and slowly the prisoners softened their hearts to him and to God.

The prisoners told Fr. Vincent about their lives working on the ships. They complained to him about how they were being treated unfairly. One day he decided to see for himself. When he boarded the ship, the captain of the ship was very friendly toward him.

"You see, Father, the faster the prisoners row, the faster the ship goes. There are still pirates who attack our ships, so it is important that our ships can sail faster than the pirate ships."

Just then, Father Vincent heard the crack of a whip. One of the prisoners who was rowing could not keep up with the others, so he was being beaten to make him row faster. Father Vincent went down to him. He could see that the man was weak and old. He told the man with the whip to unchain the prisoner and to let him row for him, in his stead. After the captain agreed, Father Vincent sat down with the other prisoners to row.

"Put the chains on me as well," Fr. Vincent told the captain.

The captain did not want to.

"Father, you are not a prisoner," explained the captain.

"I am taking the old man's place. I will not understand his suffering if I do not wear the chains like him. Put them on!" Fr. Vincent insisted.

The captain did so, shaking his head.

Fr. Vincent rowed all day long with the other prisoners. When he was unchained at the end of the day, his arms and back were on fire with pain. His ankles were raw and bleeding where the shackles had been. His skin was red and blistered from the sun. He came back the next day and did it all again. Fr. Vincent rowed for the old prisoner for months until the old man wasn't sick anymore.

Father Vincent told everyone he knew about the galley prisoners, and many people were happy to give him food and other things that the prisoners needed. Many people gave him money, so he went to work and had a hospital built for the prisoners of the galleys. Soon many people wanted to help take care of the prisoners. The king of France found out what Father Vincent was doing and made Father Vincent the Royal Priest of the Galleys.

CHAPTER 11

MISSION WORK

After some time, Father Vincent found enough people who wanted to help take care of the galley prisoners at the hospital. He felt that God was calling him back to the poor people in the country. So, that is where he went. He taught the poor in many towns about God, and always brought them food to eat. It was a lot of work for just one priest and Fr. Vincent wasn't young anymore. He was 44 years old.

One day Madame came to tell him, "Father, you cannot do all this work by yourself. You look so tired. Why don't you get some more priests to help you? You could teach them everything you know about serving God and the poor."

"I will pray about it, Madame, and if God agrees with you, He will send me some help," answered Father Vincent.

As he was praying, the face of one of the young priests who had helped him in the galleys came to his mind. Anthony had a big heart and would be a perfect mission priest. Father Vincent finished his prayers, and wrote Anthony a letter telling him about the work he was doing. After a short time young Anthony showed up to help him with a big smile on his face. Soon after that, Father Vincent found another priest named Francis who wanted to join and learn from him as well.

Madame's husband founded an old school named "School of the Good Children" for Father Vincent and his little group of priests. Madame gave Father Vincent enough money to do his mission work.

Early one morning, before the sun had come up, Father Vincent woke up the sleepy priests. "It is time to go, my friends," he said merrily.

"What time is it, Father?" young Anthony asked, rubbing his eyes.

"It's after four. We will say our prayers and be on our way," answered Father Vincent.

They dressed quickly in their simple clothes, prayed and left the school on foot.

"Why do we have to walk all the way, Father?" asked the priest named Francis; after they had gone a couple of miles.

"We will walk instead of riding horses. It will take longer, but in that time we will talk about what we are going to say to the people. We need to teach them how to live a good life, so that they will do what is pleasing to the Lord," said Father.

The priests walked all day. They looked like beggars in their simple clothes. They stopped a couple of times to eat some bread.

As it was getting dark, Father Vincent told them, "Let's look for a good place to sleep tonight."

"We are still miles from a town, Father," they told him.

"I mean a soft place on the ground, my friends. If we are going to help the poor, we need to know how they feel," he scolded the shocked men lightly. The small group of priests spent their first night on mission sleeping on the ground like beggars. The next day, the priests finally made it to the first town. They went to the church and asked the priest there if they could preach to his people.

"How much will it cost?" the church priest wanted to know. "It will cost you nothing. God's words are free," Father Vincent answered.

The church priest was happy to let them do a mission there. They had practiced what they were going to say. They taught the poor people using simple words that they could understand. Many people were eager to hear the good news about Jesus that the mission priests brought to them. After the mission, the church was packed with people who were excited about their faith.

"You can come back anytime!" the church priest told them happily as they left town.

Father Vincent and his little group of mission priests went all over the countryside for many months teaching others about the hope and love of Jesus Christ. Soon every church priest in every town wanted the mission priests to come to their town to do a mission. Father Vincent's mission priests always walked everywhere they went, slept on the ground, and took no money for their work.

Finally, at Christmas, the three mission priests walked back to Paris where they rested for a little while. Before long, everyone in France knew about Father Vincent's mission. Soon Father Vincent had enough priests who were glad to help him serve the poor.

CHAPTER 12

LOUISE

When Father Vincent got back to the school in Paris, there was a visitor waiting for him. It was a lovely young woman dressed all in black. She was crying as she sat in the cold room waiting for Fr. Vincent. Fr. Vincent knew who she was because he had met her before. Her name was Louise. He had met her in a church one day a few months earlier when he was praying for a mission priest. She was the only other person in the church with him. Then, she was dressed in black and was sobbing big tears.

Fr. Vincent had asked her, "Did someone die, my child?"

"Not yet, Father. My husband is very sick," she sobbed.

"It is God's will." Fr. Vincent assured her.

"I am afraid, Father! I don't know what I will do without my husband," she cried.

"When that time comes, come and see me at the School of the Good Children. Don't worry. God has a plan for your life," he told her.

Now seeing her again at his school, Vincent remembered his earlier words to Louise, asking her to come and see him.

"Hello, Louise. What is wrong, my dear?" he asked the crying woman.

"Oh Father! Thank God you are back!" she sobbed. "My husband has died, and I don't know what to do with myself."

Father Vincent scratched his head. "Let me think about this, my dear. For now, go home, and think about those who have less than you, like the sick and hungry people in this city. Then come back and see me again," he scolded her lightly.

Louise walked away slowly with her head down. A few weeks later, Louise came back to see Father Vincent again. She looked different. Her clothes were simple and she wore a big smile on her face.

"You were right, Father! I stopped thinking only of myself and started thinking of others. I sold my big house and all my things. I spend my days now caring for the poor people. They bring me closer to God. I am so happy! Thank you, Father Vincent!" Louise said joyfully.

"God has blessed you, my dear. I have thought about you, and I could use your help with my missions. I need someone to manage all the food that comes in for the poor. Would you like to do that?" asked Fr. Vincent.

"Nothing would make me happier, Father!" Louise cried. "Tell me what to do and I will do it!"

Louise was a big help to Father Vincent. Her zeal surprised even him. He thanked God for her every day. Louise had enough money left from her husband to live on, and she had a great number of friends who had a lot of money. She formed a group of Christian women who wanted to help the poor. They gladly gave her and

Fr. Vincent the money to buy food and clothes for them. Louise woke up at five o'clock in the morning and worked all day long. As hard as she worked, she could not do it alone. Her friends in their fancy clothes did not want to help her with the hard jobs. They did not want to get their hands dirty.

One day, a young country girl called on Father Vincent.

"How may I help you, young woman?" Father Vincent asked her as he opened the door.

Fr. Vincent was dressed so simply that the girl did not think he was an important priest.

"Good day, sir. My name is Margaret. I am looking for Father Vincent. I believe that God is calling me to help him serve the poor. I am a hard worker from the country. I am strong, and I don't mind doing the jobs that nobody else wants to do. I don't need any pay. I just want to serve Jesus and the poor. Can you ask Fr. Vincent if he could use my help, please?" she pleaded.

Father Vincent's eye twinkled. He could not believe his ears. This girl could be the answer to his prayers. She seemed to be exactly what Louise needed.

"Come in, Miss Margaret," Father Vincent said, opening the door.

CHAPTER 13

THE LITTLE SISTERS

Louise was delighted to have Margaret help her in the missions. One day when Fr. Vincent was visiting them, Louise told him, "Father, Margaret is perfect for the job. She is so sweet to everyone and doesn't mind washing all the dirty clothes and dishes. She also enjoys teaching the poor children how to read! If only you could find more girls like her for me," added Louise hopefully.

Soon Father Vincent found more hard working country girls who wanted to help serve the poor like Margaret. Louise was like a mother to them. She taught them, "It is not only our job to bring soup to the poor, but we must remember to do it with the love of God."

The little group of girls became known as the Little Sisters. To pray, to work and to obey were their rules. Their life was hard. They woke up at four in the morning, ate plain food, worked in dirty places and were always tired. Father Vincent met with them once a week and taught them how to live their faith.

"Above all things, be humble and simple. Go where you are needed, but do not stay to chat. Walk with your eyes down when you are in the streets so no one will look at you. Suffer and be strong. If a hungry person knocks on your door, and you are saying your prayers, stop praying and feed him. The poor are our pathway to heaven, and we can never do too much for them," he said. The Little Sisters worked in the hospitals of Paris caring for the sick. They were also called to other towns all over France. Not a day went by when they were not asked to help somewhere.

There was a war in France in 1656, and the king asked for the Little Sisters to come and care for the hurt soldiers. Louise sent four of her sisters to help the soldiers. Even the Little Sisters were shocked to see how filthy and sick the soldiers were. The Little Sisters rarely complained but cared for the soldiers with joy in their hearts. Two of the Sisters got sick while there and died. When Louise got the news about the two Sisters that had died, she asked four more sisters to go to take their places. All

SAINT VINCENT, FRIEND OF THE POOR

four of them happily agreed. They were eager to do God's will.

Then the plague hit France hard. Beggars were found dead in the streets. Hospitals were so full that they had to turn people away. The Little Sisters seemed to never rest. Even Louise's rich friends came to help the Sisters care for the sick and dying. Little Margaret was the first to die. She let a sick woman share her bed at the hospital. The woman got better, but little Margaret became ill and died a few days later.

Louise worked side by side with her girls. She tended the sick, prayed with the dying, and closed the eyes of the dead. She became pale and thin herself. Then one day the plague went away as fast as it had come.

CHAPTER 14

THE ORPHANS

The Thirty Year War in France brought hunger, sickness and much crime. It was not safe to walk the streets of Paris. People had left farms and small towns, and went to the city to find food. Often, the children suffered the most. Many were left by their parents because they could not afford to feed them. Father Vincent was deeply troubled by this.

By this time, almost everyone in France knew who Father Vincent was because he had helped so many people. He had rich friends and poor friends. He saw Jesus in everyone he met. He walked with a limp because of his old arrow wound. He wore a brown cape and always had a twinkle in his dark brown eyes.

One day when he was limping down the street, a woman dressed in rags came up to him. She was carrying a tiny baby in her arms.

She said to Father Vincent, "Please take my baby. I know you will take good care of him. He will die of hunger if I keep him."

She ran off crying before Father Vincent could say anything. He looked down at the tiny boy. His hand was the size of Father Vincent's thumb.

"So God is giving me another job," he sighed.

He carried the baby home and baptized him. Then he took the baby to the Little Sisters.

Louise opened the door.

"Look what I have found, Louise. I baptized him," grinned Fr. Vincent.

"Oh no, Father," Louise said sadly, "we already have so many that we can barely feed them. Take him to the Couche."

Father Vincent was heartbroken. The Couche was an awful place. An old widow woman took in about four hundred children a year there, but none of them lived very long.

So Father Vincent said, "Call a meeting with your rich friends today. We will work something out."

At the meeting Father Vincent brought in the baby for the women to see. "Is there anyone here," he said as he passed the baby around for each woman to hold, "who can afford to help this poor child of God? Louise needs a little more money to feed this baby. If we don't take care of him, he will surely die. Jesus told us to bring the little children to him. Can we send a baby away when God has sent him to us?"

All of the women started to cry. Every one of them gave the Little Sisters a large sum of money. They even had enough to buy a bigger house, so that they could take in more children who had been left by their parents.

The king of France found out about the orphans and even he gave the Little Sisters a large amount of money. Father Vincent and the Little Sisters used the money to save the children at the Couche. Father Vincent would visit the orphans at any hour of the day, and he knew them all by name. Children were cared for, baptized and schooled. Many of the orphans became priests and nuns when they were older. It went on that way for a long time, even after Father Vincent died.

CHAPTER 15

THE LAST DAYS

Even in the last days of his life, Father Vincent woke up at four in the morning. He spent the first hours at prayer, and then spent the rest of the day helping others. He was in pain all the time at the end of his life. His feet became so sore that he could hardly walk. It was mostly due to the time he had spent trading places with the galley prisoner on the rowing ship. The chains left terrible sores on his ankles which never fully healed.

Because Father Vincent was so old and weak, he had to allow himself to have the fireplace lit in his room and an extra blanket on his bed each night. One of the queen's friends liked Father Vincent very much, and she had a gift sent to him one day when he was over seventy years old. She knew he would not like it because he was so humble, but she also knew that he needed it. She even had the queen write him a letter telling him to take it.

When Father Vincent saw the carriage outside his house, he asked the driver,

"What is this for?"

"It is a gift for you," the driver said as he handed the letter from the queen to him.

Father Vincent humbly obeyed the queen and took the gift, but he was not happy about it.

"I am just a peasant. What do I need this fancy thing for? It is a disgrace!" Father Vincent told the driver.

Father Vincent only used the carriage when his feet were so painful that he could not walk. He would visit the poor people and often he would drive them around in it while he talked with them. He also lent his carriage to whoever needed it. Soon "Father Vincent's carriage" was well known all over Paris.

A couple of months before Father Vincent died, Louise got very sick. He told her in a letter before she passed away, "You are going a little before me, but I will meet you very soon in heaven." He could not go to see her because he had a very high fever. During the next two months he would slowly limp with his crutches to mass in great pain. He could not say the mass himself anymore. Then he would go back to his room, sit at a little table, and welcome anyone who wanted to see him. He helped others until the end.

During the last few days of his life, Father Vincent was in pain all night and could hardly get any sleep on his hard straw bed. He still had a sweet smile on his face in the morning. The only thing he said when he was in pain was, "My Jesus, my dear Jesus."

In September 1660, Father Vincent fell asleep in his chair. He was awakened, and he quietly whispered, "I trust." With these words on his lips, he gently gave up his soul to the Lord.

EPILOGUE

Father Vincent was made a saint in the year 1737 by Pope Clement XII. His feast day is September 27. He is known as the saint of charity because he did so many good things for so many people. Eight miracles of healing have been attributed to him. The Mission Priests now go by the name of the Lazarists, and they have 3,600 members. The Little Sisters became known as the Sisters of Charity and are still hard at work today serving the poor with 27,200 sisters in eighty different countries. The Society of Saint Vincent De

Paul has 875,000 church members in 130 countries. Father Vincent believed in the virtue of action. He said that lengthy prayer should come before action to make sure it was God's will. "Perfection comes from doing the will of God," he added.

ABOUT THE AUTHOR

Kim Varela lives on the Western Slope of Colorado with her husband, Dennis and four of her children. She enjoys caring for her children and farm animals. She was born in Roseville, California. Later she moved to Dallas, Texas where she taught bilingual education and met Dennis. They moved to Colorado after marrying in 1999. Kim likes reading books about the Catholic faith and the saints. St. Vincent, Friend of the Poor is her first book.

Made in the USA
Lexington, KY
03 September 2014